I REBUKE YOU DEVIL!

Don't Touch My Body!

By Acillen K. Watts

I Rebuke You Devil!

Don't Touch My Body!

For information contact:
info@acillen.com
www.acillen.com

ISBN: 9798841416036
First Edition: July 2022

10 9 8 7 6 5 4 3 2 1

You are very special and
Jesus loves you very much.
He wants you to be happy
and safe from harm. If
someone is bad to you,
touches your body, or asks
you to touch their private
parts, always tell someone.
Do not be afraid because
God is always with you. You
have more power than you
know.

God created a beautiful world filled with nice people who love Jesus, but the bible tells us we have an enemy called the devil who causes people to sin.

The devil is very bad.

Sadly, there are people who are filled with bad spirits from the devil. They hurt children and trick them into doing things they should not do.
1 John 3:7-8

Moms and dads should always do their best to take good care of their children.

They are supposed to love them, protect them, and keep them safe from harm.

Your mom and dad, or whoever looks after you, should always warn you about bad people who might try to hurt you.

Some children do not have
good moms and dads who
show them love and care.
That is not their fault. They
did nothing wrong.

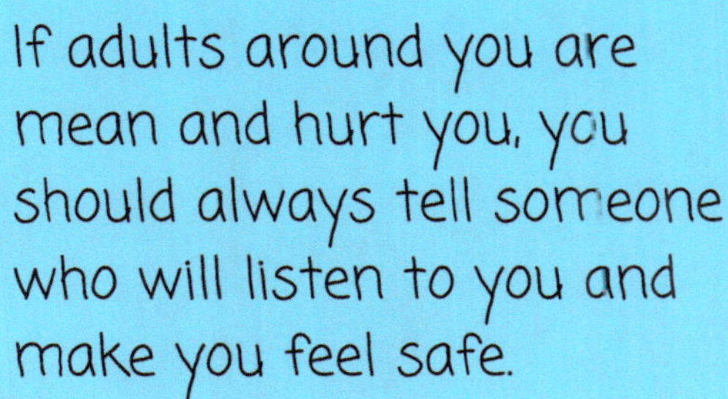

If adults around you are
mean and hurt you, you
should always tell someone
who will listen to you and
make you feel safe.

When they hurt you, they might tell you not to tell anyone because they don't want anyone to know they are doing bad things to you.

They might tell you no one will believe you or say if you tell they will do something really bad to you or someone you love..

First, agree not to tell anyone. Then run and tell an adult you trust as soon as you can!

People should not touch you on your private parts and they should not make you touch them on their private parts, with any part of your body. The red X shows where people should not rub or touch you.

You should always tell someone you trust if someone hurts you or touches your private parts with their hands or other objects.

Girls have body parts made especially for them by God. No one should play with your body, it is not a toy.

Boys have body parts made special for them by God too. No one should ever touch or tickle your private areas or cause them to hurt.

Some bad people may try to get you to play a game with them where they touch your body in places they should not.

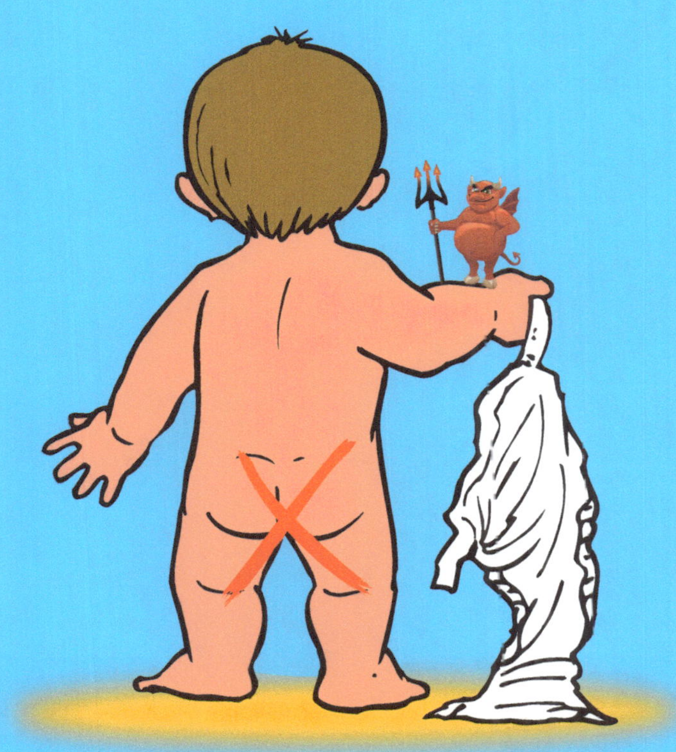

That is not a real game. Only a very bad person will try to scare you into doing things that make you feel dirty. You can tell them "NO, I rebuke you devil. Don't touch my body!"

No one should ever ask you to bend over so they can touch your toush (butt) or between your legs.

No one should rub on your private parts. Your body is special. If someone tries to rub on you in these areas, tell an adult that makes you feel safe.

Bath time is special.

An adult who makes
you feel safe is the
only person who
should help you at
bath time.

When you are big
enough, you can bathe
yourself and close the
door for privacy.

Bring your clothes in
the bathroom with
you. Only come out
when you have all of
your clothes on.

Babies and toddlers need help getting dressed until they can dress themselves.

If someone helps you get your clothes on, they should not rub on your private parts or make you feel ashamed.

If someone makes you feel uncomfortable, ask them to leave the room. Tell them you can do it on your own.

Potty time is very important.

Someone who makes you feel safe may need to help you when you are too little.

If you can use the bathroom by yourself at home, go in alone and wipe your bottom until there is nothing left on the tissue.

Never go into any public bathroom alone.. A bad person could be waiting inside. Get an adult you trust to stand near your door.

If someone touches or plays with your private parts while helping you in the bathroom, say, "No. I rebuke you devil!"

Tell someone else you can trust and show them where the bad person touched you. Do not wait. Tell as soon as you can.

Bedtime should be safe for you. Always say your prayers and ask God to keep you safe through the night.

When you lay down, you can be tucked in and get a great big hug! No one should come into your room while you sleep and touch your body. Sweet Dreams!

Close your eyes and
sleep peacefully in the
safety of Jesus' arms.

If an adult or child sleeps in the same bed as you, do not let them touch your private parts. If they do, tell them you don't like that. Then tell an adult who makes you feel safe. Do not sleep with bad children or adults.

Do not be afraid or ashamed. Pray to God and rebuke the devil in Jesus' name. Remember Jesus loves you.

Little girls and boys should not sit on a stranger's lap, not even if he is dressed up as a Santa Clause.

Mom and dad can cuddle with you in the chair, but if you are uncomfortable, tell them you want to sit in your own chair.

It is alright to sit in a big chair by yourself. It is nice and comfy.

If someone you don't know tries to take you with them,
yell as loud as you can and fight with all your might.

Scream "Leave me alone. Stranger, stranger, help me!"
You can even yell FIRE to get someone's attention!

Never tell a stranger your name, your school, or where you live. Bad people may try to take you away from your family and hurt you.

If someone bothers you or another child, tell an adult who makes you feel safe so they can protect you.

If a stranger asks you to help them find their dog or child or offers you candy or ice cream, never go with them. They are bad people. Yell loud so someone can hear you say, "I rebuke you devil! Leave me alone!"

If someone makes you feel afraid, pray and say, "I rebuke you devil, in the name of Jesus. Be sure to stay away from them if you can.

If a big person is bullying and being super mean to you, even if you know them, you must tell the truth to someone who can help you.

Always ask God to lead you to someone who will help you.

The devil is always busy. Even when you are having fun, he is looking for ways to hurt God's children.

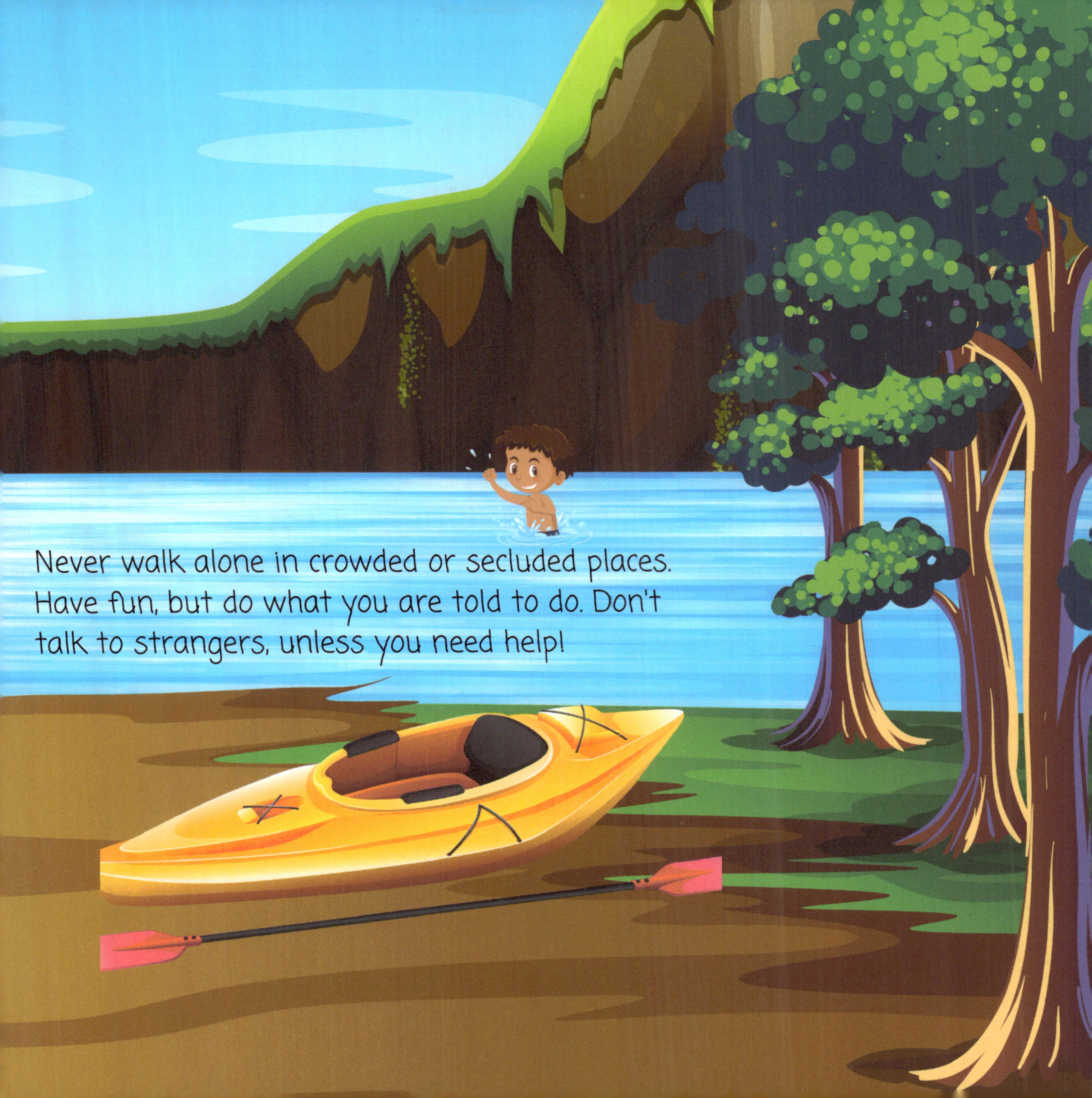
Never walk alone in crowded or secluded places. Have fun, but do what you are told to do. Don't talk to strangers, unless you need help!

When you are out with an adult you trust, be sure to stay close to them. Always be on the lookout for danger.

If someone in your family is the one hurting you, tell someone as soon as you can. NEVER keep a bad secret. You matter to God. He would want you to tell the truth.

If a friend or someone you love is being hurt, help them. Let an adult you trust know about it, EVEN if the person doesn't want you to tell anyone!

Big brothers and sisters, or any person older than you, should not be mean to you. They should never touch your private parts or do bad things to your body.

If they ask you to touch their private parts or make you feel uncomfortable about your body, always tell an adult.

Big brothers and sisters should be nice to you and protect you from bad people who want to hurt you. They should spend time with you and show you love.

If you are sitting alone waiting for someone to pick you up, never talk to or go with a stranger.
If you are lost, pray and ask a police officer or store owner to help you.

If someone is hurting your body, you might feel scared because they are bigger than you. You can be brave and rebuke the devil.

Don't let the bad person keep hurting you or someone else. Try your best to tell someone so you can be helped.

If you can't tell your mom or dad if someone touches you in a bad way, tell grandma and grandpa when someone hurts you. Bad people can be male or female, so always be careful.

No matter who the bad person who hurts you is, you have to tell someone who can help you.

If you tell someone, but they don't believe you, or won't listen to you, tell someone else until you find the person who will believe you.

If someone close to you is hurting your body, you might feel sad for telling on them. You have to tell the truth so they can stop doing bad things to you.

Some days you might feel sad and feel like no one loves you, but that is not true. You are special and you deserve to be a child, free to live in safety and have fun.

Your body is God's creation. No one should make you feel sad or icky because they are touching your private parts or making you touch their private parts.

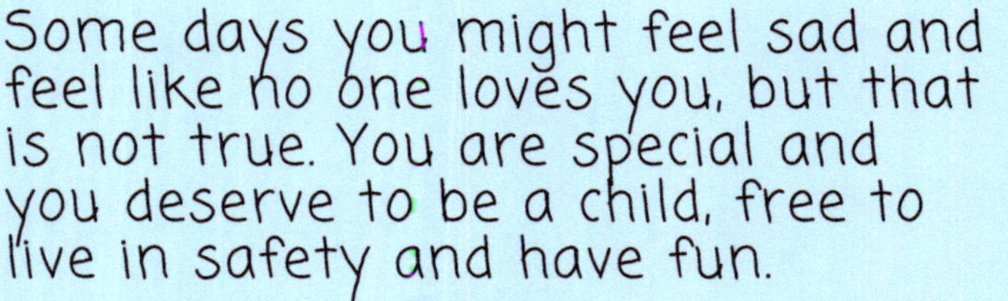

ALWAYS TELL SOMEONE NO MATTER HOW AFRAID YOU ARE.

PRAYER

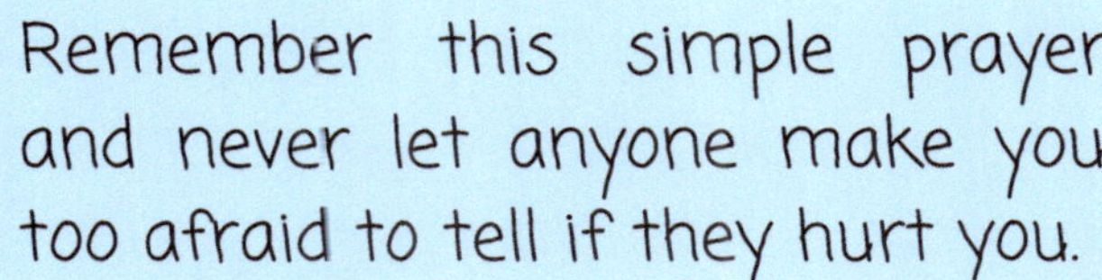

Remember this simple prayer and never let anyone make you too afraid to tell if they hurt you.

Dear Lord, thank you for loving me. Please put a hedge of protection around me to keep me safe. Help me to be strong and brave. Make me invisible to the devil. Have mercy on me and don't let my enemies hurt me. In Jesus' name, I pray. Amen.

1 John 3:7-8

7 Little children, let no one deceive you. Whoever practices righteousness is righteous, as he is righteous. 8 Whoever makes a practice of sinning is of the devil, for the devil has been sinning from the beginning. The reason the Son of God appeared was to destroy the works of the devil.